Guide For Quick Fixes For Laptops And Cell Phones

By Bob Brunelle

Guide For Quick Fixes For Laptops and Cell Phones

by Bob Brunelle

Table of Contents

1. Introduction

I want to thank you for purchasing our 54 Bit Magnetic Driver Kit, and Precision Screwdriver Set.

What good is a tool set if you don't know how to fix anything? We have included some quick fixes for laptops and cell phones.

Laptop Repairs:

Do you own a laptop that is constantly being moved around? Does your work have you traveling with your laptop. The days of the PC are pretty much over. A laptop gets a lot more punishment than desktops do. With this in mind, notebook manufacturers manufacture their systems to stand up from shaking and occasional drops.

Despite the way they are made, laptops are often quick to show signs of wear and tear -- and not just on the outside. Most people have their whole life on their laptops. If your laptop is damaged it can cost you time and money in lost of valuable information and productivity.

Thankfully, your laptop or notebooks can often be cured with a quick fix.

To pinpoint the most common problems, we picked the brains of senior technical-support officials at some major computer manufacturers. And we've provided solutions for getting your laptop back up and running with minimal effort.

Cell Phones:

Dropping your cell phone, spilling water on it, overheating the battery accidents can happen, and they're not always your fault. How you choose to repair those accidents is your choice.

We would like to share some of their favorite at-home solutions, that cell phone specialist recommend. These tips are for pros and beginners.

iPhones, smart phones and cell phones with broken screens, water damage and charging failures tend to affect the majority of the repairs required..

They are also the most visible problems and can be diagnosed somewhat
more easily; so we'll focus on these problems first!

---

2. Laptop Overheating

1. Overheating
Symptom: crashes, freezes

Solution: Clean out air vents, put filtered material over the inhalation vent, or update BIOS

Overheating can rob your laptop of performance and often cause a host of system crashes and freezing. Every computer generates lots of heat, but laptops are especially susceptible to overheating due to their small size and lack of ventilation. Excessive dust can clog air vents and deprive your system of cold air to cool off the CPU. You can often solve overheating issues simply by cleaning out these air vents with a cloth or keyboard cleaner.

To prevent further dust buildup, place a piece of filtered cloth, like a cheese cloth over the inhalation vent. Don't place one over the exhaust vent, as that's where hot air is supposed to flow out of the system quickly. If the cloth doesn't work, you may want to update your system's BIOS, which controls the laptop's hardware. Most manufacturers offer an installation file that updates BIOS files automatically, which often address heat management. Just make sure that your notebook is connected to the power supply when updating the BIOS.

3. Slow Hard Drive

Slow Hard Drive:

Symptom: Excessive program load times, slow file transfers

Solution: Disk defragg or defragmentation

Disorganized information on your hard drive can slow performance because the computer requires more time to sift through data fragments and bad sectors on the drive. This problem can be cleared up easily (but not especially quickly; defragging can sometimes take hours) using the built-in Windows tool called Disk Defragmenter. You can access this program through the Programs menu in the Accessories or System Tools folder. Simply click the Analyze button to see if your disk drive requires defragmenting, and then click Defragment to begin.

Other options include the free Power Defragmenter, and Diskeeper 2007 which offers more features like complete automation, real-time defragmenting, and InvisiTasking technology, which allows Diskeeper to run in the background without draining resources.

4. Need More Memory

Need More Memory:

Symptom: Sluggish performance when using multiple applications, hangups, excessive boot up time

Solution: Upgrade your RAM, try a (ReadyBoost-enabled) USB drive

If your laptop takes a long time to boot up, you may want to conduct an audit of your startup programs. To do this, place your cursor over the icons in the task bar at the bottom right of the screen. If you rarely use any of these programs, right-click and disable them. To take more control over what programs load when you boot up, download System Suite 7 Professional (there may be a cos)t which includes, among 60 powerful tools, a startup manager and optimizer.

Should you need to purchase a new memory chip, Kingston (www.kingston.com) and Crucial (www.crucial.com) offer tools on their Web sites for determining which products are compatible with your notebook. You can also try www.4allmemory.com.

5. Bad Keyboard:

Bad Keyboard:

Symptom: Loose or Missing Keys

Solution: Replace keyboard

Keyboards get the brunt of abuse on any laptop, either from typing or spilled coffee. As a result, keys can often become dislodged or worn out. Thankfully, laptop makers provide quick on line guides for replacing keyboards on their support pages; simply type "keyboard replacement" into the search bar or check the manufacturer's knowledge base.

For instance, Toshiba's "Ask Iris" document database provides hardware-replacement guides. To remove the old keyboard, you'll typically just have to remove some screws from the bottom of the laptop and unlock the keyboard with a button or snap mechanism, which secures it to the frame. Replacement keyboards are usually covered under warranty or can be purchased relatively cheaply. Dell, for example, sells them for $15 to $25. The company also offers plastic keyboard protectors for $10 to $15 on its Web site. CompuCoveroffers keyboard protectors for a variety of other laptops.

6. Hard Drive Failure

Hard Drive Failure:

Symptom: Loud clicking sounds whenever the computer accesses data from the hard drive

Solution: On line backup sites, replace hard drive

Obviously, the best defense against a hard drive crash is a good backup solution. These days, plenty of options abound, but among software solutions, we like Norton Save & Restore 2.0 (There may be a charge) for its ease of use.

If you're going to back up your data on line, go with Carbonite, which backs up your system automatically and tracks changes in the background without hogging precious system resources. Even if you go the online route, a hard drive failure will bring your notebook or laptop to its knees.

Fortunately, a number of tools can test your drive for problems. If hard drive replacement becomes necessary, be sure to back up as much data as possible and then switch out the hard drive. You can find step-by-step directions for the replacement procedure on most manufacturers' support sites. For instance, Lenovo is the laptop I have they go the extra mile with videos showing the replacement process; type "replacement movie" on www.lenovo.com to check it out.

If you want to preserve the data on your old drive and make switching to a new one as painless as possible, we recommend Apricorn's EZ Upgrade Universal & Hard Drive Upgrade Bundle. Available in 40GB, 80GB, 100GB, and 120GB capacities, and ranging in price from $109 to $149, this kit enables you to upgrade your hard drive in three steps. The package includes cloning and backup software, and it lets you use your old hard drive for backup purposes-- assuming it still works.

7. Can't Connect to Wireless Network

Can't Connect to Wireless Network:

Symptom: No Internet connection, frequent time-outs while Web browsing

Solution: Make sure wireless is turned on, smarter software tools, make sure router is broadcasting network name (SSID)

Part of taking your laptop everywhere on the go is expecting to be able to connect to any wireless network, whether in an airport, coffee shop, or hotel. But wireless networks, by their very nature, are finicky beasts. Some laptops come with an external button or switch, separate from the software settings, to enable wireless connectivity. Always make sure this wireless toggle is switched on. Also make sure that the network you're connecting to is broadcasting its network name or SSID.

If you'd rather steer clear of networking issues altogether, or want a tool to help you troubleshoot without having to learn any lingo, download an all-in-one utility like Network Magic (Their may be a small cost). It helps you easily set up and secure your network, complete with a comprehensive network map, as well as repair broken wireless Internet connections. Road warriors should consider JiWire's Hotspot Helper (There may be a small cost), which will not only show where you can log on via Wi-Fi but also will protect your privacy while you surf the Web wirelessly. In addition, this utility offers secure e-mail delivery, just like you get back in the office.

8. Outdated Video Drivers

Outdated Video Drivers:

Symptom: Garbled or distorted video

Solution: Download the latest drivers

Video issues are a common complaint among notebook users. The trouble often stems from newer games and software that require the latest video card drivers to work. Even though most laptops ship with the latest driver files, some systems will be outdated by the time the machine is sold. That's why it's critical to update your video card's drivers frequently--sometimes the audio and network drivers may need to be updated as well.

Many notebook manufacturers offer installation packs that will give you the latest drivers and offer automated tools to update the rest of your notebook. Lenovo, for example, hosts its driver files at lenovo.com/support. Alienware tests new drivers for all its machines and hosts them in the support area of its Web site. However, if you fail to find drivers at your notebook manufacturer's site, you can try the video card's manufacturer, usually ATI or Nvidia. If your system comes with an integrated graphics chip from Intel, your best bet is the laptop manufacturer's website, although you can also try Intel's support and downloads page.

9. Virus or Spyware Infestation

Virus or Spyware Infestation:

Symptom: Excessive pop ups, slow downloads

Solution: Install anti spyware programs, use free virus scans

Nothing can cripple your system like malware. The first line of defense is always prevention. It's best to have a subscription to a service like Norton 360 ($79per year). Norton impressed us with this unobtrusive security suite that offers stellar antivirus and spyware protection, file backups, and performance tuning without a complex user interface. The Norton suite also offers a firewall option that will silently block most threats while alerting the user to friendly programs requesting Web access.

If you don't want to spend any money, you can bolster your defenses with free tools like Ad-Awareand Spybot: Search and Destroy. While both are excellent tools, each has its own strengths and weaknesses--Spybot is better at tracking down malicious code like pop-ups, while Ad-Aware does a better job removing cookies (text files that advertisers copy to a user's computer to track surfing habits). We recommend scheduling periodic scans with both of these tools, just to be safe.

If these tools fail to locate a virus, you may want to try Trend Micro's free House Call at housecall.trendmicro.com, which is sometimes more adept at identifying viruses than other programs. Trend Micro also offers a free database of viruses and manual removal tips, if automated solutions fail.

10. Stuck Pixels

Stuck Pixels:

Symptom: Green or red dots on your notebook's screen

Solution: Massage away dead pixels

Nonconforming or stuck pixels can be a nuisance on an otherwise functional laptop LCD. The pixels usually remain green or red without lighting up properly with the other pixels on the display. Unfortunately, manufacturers will not replace an LCD for just one or two stuck pixels; in fact, some require as many as 10 to 18 dead pixels before they'll take action.

There is a solution, though. Take a soft material, like a felt cloth, and gently rub in a circular motion around the stuck pixel. Performing this trick will usually get the pixel to light up properly. Once you find the right location and pressure to illuminate the pixel, hold your finger there for up to two minutes, and voila, no more stuck pixel.

11. Battery Won't Hold a Charge

Battery Won't Hold a Charge:

Symptom: Your laptop or notebook runs only a few minutes when unplugged

Solution: Battery replacement

Over their lifespans, lithium-ion batteries can lose the ability to hold a charge. After a few years, some batteries will last only a fraction of the rated runtime. Replacing a battery is relatively simple; most pop out from the bottom or back of the laptop.

Many retailers, however, charge hundreds of dollars for a new battery. Sites like batteries.com specialize in discount laptop batteries and can save you money on a brand new battery for your laptop. The company even offers a two-year warranty and 45-day money-back guarantee on all laptop-battery orders.

12. System Crash

System Crash:

Symptom: Notebook won't boot up

Solution: Remove the hard drive and place it into an external enclosure. Run Checkdisk.

Most people go into panic mode when their computers refuse to boot up. More often than not, however, the problem is as simple as a missing system file or a bad sector on the hard drive. To determine if that's the case, you can remove your hard drive using the instructions from the manufacturer and place the drive into a USB enclosure--these are external housings for internal hardware. You can find them at most retailers like Best Buy, Staples, or Newegg, for less than $40.

Next, connect the enclosure's USB cable to an open USB port on a working PC. If the file system is still intact, the hard drive should show up as an external drive and allow you to transfer data to and from the drive. Next, try running Checkdisk on the drive by opening a DOS prompt (Start/Programs/Accessories/Command Prompt) and typing in X: where X is the letter of your external drive. Then hit Enter. Now type "chkdsk /f." Your system may ask you to dismount the drive; this is okay, so type Y and then hit Enter.

Your notebook will now display some information about your drive (file system type and serial number) and then scan the drive, fixing any errors it encounters. An error report will print out, so you can see what changes were made to the drive. If all went well, you'll be good to go once you plug the hard drive back into the crashed notebook and power it on.

13. Opening Your Cell Phone and Putting You Cell Phone Back Together

Opening Your Cell Phone:

First: Turn off the cell phone and remove the battery. Unless your cell phone is experiencing a software problem, the difficulties with your device often stem from a broken internal component. Some handsets come apart easily, while others need a lot of tinkering with. Consulting your user manual or on line resources (videos, discussion forums, etc.) is a good second step. Just like any kind of surgery, a sterile environment is best. Your cell phone isn't going to pick up an infection, but the slightest amount of debris could get into the circuitry and cause more problems. A little bit of patience is as good as having an assistant nearby. You'll let yourself concentrate and not become so frustrated if something goes wrong.

Putting You Cell Phone Back Together:

Before you take your cell phone apart, make sure you know how to put it back together again. Some devices require heating up components so

they release from the parts they're assembled to. Make sure you don't damage parts and components when disassembling them, especially when they are glued or otherwise adhered to one another, or else they will not reassemble. Parts and components within the device need to
be reset exactly as they were. As compact and feature-rich as cell phones are, they leave no room for error.

14. Water Damage

Water Damage:

Puddles, toilets and other pools of water have claimed the lives of countless cell phones. We all dread it will happen to our devices. If you are so unfortunate, our specialists have a few tips for trying to revive your phone. Water and other liquids can enter your phone
through seams in the case, such as by the screen or battery, or through the micro-USB port and other openings. Just a little exposure can be as damaging as dunking it in a pool.

Common Forms of Damage Short Circuits:

Liquids such as water are conductive and will wreck havoc on the circuitry inside the phone. Electricity follows the path of least resistance, which is why touching a live electrical wire while you are grounded will result in a nasty shock. Water seeps between the gaps in the circuitry and, being conductive, allows electrical signals to jump to a nearby, more attractive destination rather than following the paths provided by the phone's circuit board. The circuit has been cut short; or, a "short circuit" has formed.
Short circuits are caused when two components inside the phone that are not supposed
to interact do interact because the water has allowed electricity to conduct between them.

Usually, cell phones have no safeguards to protect against short circuits.

Corrosion:

Another type of damage is more long-term than the immediate effects of a short circuit. Rust is caused by water coming into contact with metal, and then this metal is exposed to air, which corrodes the metal through oxidation. Rusty metals are not as conductive for electricity as a clean, polished surface. Cell phone charging ports, internal circuitry and other components rely heavily on metallic connections and copper wiring. Corrosion
affects cell phones just as much as it does any other electronic device.

Other:

Contrary to popular belief, you cannot "fry" a cell phone by exposing it to water. You won't find any smoke coming out of your device any time soon.

Solutions:

Besides accidents, a lot of people imagine a cell phone vibrating in a drinking glass when they think of water damage. It's true, if you place a cell phone in a glass, there's a good chance that it will continue working while it's soaked in liquid. A popular remedy is to fill a plastic bag or covered container full of rice, insert the cell phone, and surround it with the grains. The idea is that the rice will absorb the liquid. Your cell phone may work for a while after that, but maybe not for long. Without proper airflow, the liquid doesn't go very far and enough of it can linger inside the cell phone, and corrode the internal components.

Solutions Continued:

Leaving the device in the sun or letting it dry in another natural way will still invite corrosion to take over. So will taking canned air or some other kind of air blower and using it to push the liquid out. Pouring rubbing alcohol or another quick-drying household cleaner into the cell phone has some pluses and minuses as well. Liquid trapped in the phone may mix with the alcohol and evaporate, but absolutely no kind of liquid is meant to enter your phone. Household cleaners can eat away parts or cause more damage, anyways. Opening the cell phone and cleaning the interior is the only complete way to fix water damage. Please turn off the cell phone before you do so.

15. Cell Phone Cracked or Broken Screen

Cell Phone Cracked or Broken Screen:

Varying degrees of damage can exist on a cell phone's screen, from a minor fracture to what looks like a puncture wound. A lot of people can live with a small divot or crack on their device's screen without it affecting them. Let's be honest, repairs aren't always cheap and parts are expensive. Bigger issues are not so easy to live with. Glass gradually chipping away will expose sensitive regions on the phone, components beneath the glass can break, and a broken touchscreen can render a smart phone completely useless.

Solutions:
Cell phone screens include the glass, digitizer, lights and a lot of other small components. On some touchscreen devices, the factory fuses all of these parts together because it means that they can manufacture the phones faster. Instead of just replacing the glass, you now need to replace the entire screen assembly, which includes correctly attaching it to the phone's motherboard. Proper knowledge of your particular device and how it was manufactured is key to performing the correct screen repairs. The majority of repairs (for broken screens and other

problems) require opening your device, so we have included some tips for that at the end of this guide. Before beginning, turn off the cell phone!

Replacing the Glass & Other Components:

If the glass covering your mobile device's screen broke, and it is not fused to the screen assembly, you may be in some luck. Cheap replacement glass is available on line, as well as video tutorials for many different models. Likely, you will
need to use a suction to pull the glass from the screen. Use care when reapplying the glass so it looks flawless. Lights and digitizers beneath the glass can be more troublesome to repair or replace. Lights can be soldered or screwed to other pieces, including the motherboard; while digitizers are often wired to the device's computer. Once again, use care, being especially careful not to damage other parts of the phone.

Fused Touch screens:

How the touchscreen is attached to the device is up to manufacturer. Likely, you will need a suction device or a small screwdriver to remove the screen assembly. The digitizer will be linked to the cell phone's computer with a flex cable. Take careful note of how the touchscreen is positioned in the device before you proceed with extraction.

16. Battery Failure

Battery Failure:

Batteries power every cell phone on the market, from basic candy bar-shaped devices to flagship touchscreen devices. And through all the transformations cell phones have gone through, their batteries haven't changed much at all. Some of the signs your battery is going bad are longer charge times, or the cell phone loses power quicker than it used to. If you open the battery cover, you may find the battery misshapen, leaking or covered in a dried film. Most cell phones allow you to access the battery, but not all. Some are built with a "unibody" design, without a battery cover.

Solutions:

Test your battery by connecting a different charger. If there are still problems, replace the battery. Simple enough! If a new battery produces the same results as the old one and acts as though it's failing as well, it's likely a problem with the cell phone. The charging port can be easily damaged from accidentally tripping on a cord while it's connected, or through corrosion from water damage. If so, shut down the phone and prepare to explore its insides.

17. Misc Problems and Solutions

Misc Problems and Solutions:

If your cell phone is experiencing problems with the audio, slow performance or other difficulties, there are diagnostic tools built into the device that can help. For example, dialing * 3001#12345# * on the iPhone will display "Field Test," which is the phone's diagnostic mode. Here, you can test each part of the phone's functions. Here are a few more codes (may not work on all models):

BlackBerry: TEST HTC: *#*#3423#*#* iPhone: * 3001#12345# *
LG: 2945#*# or 2945*#01*# Motorola: ##7764726
Nokia: ##3282 Samsung: * #0011# Sony: 904059+>

If, indeed, it is a hardware problem that is affecting your phone, then you will need to open the device to repair or replace the appropriate parts and components.

I hope this has helped you keep your laptops, notebooks and cell phones fined tuned.

Please look for more of my products on Amazon under BJM INVESTMENTS LLC.

Thanks from all of us.

www.ingramcontent.com/pod-product-compliance
Lightning Source LLC
LaVergne TN
LVHW052126070326
832902LV00038B/3963